Little Dog

BY ALYSSA KREKELBERG

Little dog runs on the grass.

Little dog rolls in the grass.

Little dog jumps up.

Little dog sits down.

Little dog looks for squirrels.

Little dog plays with a stick.

Little dog plays with a ball.

Little dog plays with a toy.

Little dog eats its food.

Little dog sleeps.

Note to Caregivers and Educators

Sight words are a foundation for reading. It's important for young readers to have sight words memorized at a glance without breaking them down into individual letter sounds. Sight words are often phonetically irregular and can't be sounded out, so readers need to memorize them. Knowing sight words allows readers to focus on more difficult words in the text. The intent of this book is to repeat specific sight words as many times as possible throughout the story. Through repetition of the words, emerging readers will recognize, and ideally memorize, each sight word. Memorizing sight words can help improve readers' literacy skills.

dog
little

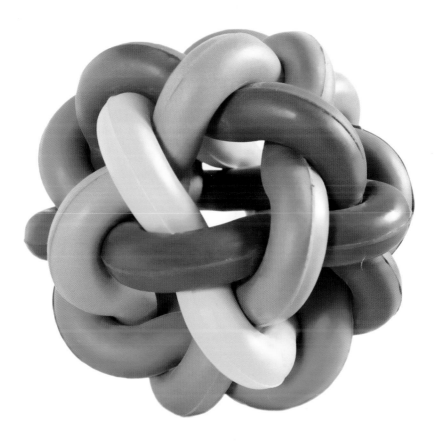

About the Author

Alyssa Krekelberg is a children's book editor and author. She lives in Minnesota and enjoys exploring the great outdoors with her hyper husky.

Published by The Child's World®
1980 Lookout Drive • Mankato, MN 56003-1705
800-599-READ • www.childsworld.com

Photographs ©: Bigandt Photography/iStockphoto, cover, 1, 3; Ken Griffiths/iStockphoto, 4, 11; iStockphoto, 7, 12, 15, 16, 19, 20; Bigandt.com/Shutterstock Images, 8; Debra Millet/iStockphoto, 23

ISBN 9781503835641
LCCN 2019943123

Printed in the United States of America

3 1333 04903 7649